DNA

OF A
REVOLUTION

The Small Group Experience

Response to DNA of a Revolution

GARY has been helping churches recalibrate ministry for well over 20 years now. Here in this book he gives us a simple and straightforward way to connect with the energies that propelled the original church. DNA of a Revolution is a meaningful addition to the global conversation from the director of ChurchNext at CRM.

— **ALAN HIRSCH**
AUTHOR // ACTIVIST // DREAMER // WWW.ALANHIRSCH.ORG

FOR much of my pastoral life, I've been looking for a book like this. Gary extracts the essential values of a living movement of Jesus followers and captures the timeless relevance of the early church in Acts. The first church was not perfect, but by flexibly following the Holy Spirit, these everyday disciples changed the world.

— **TIM ERICKSON**
SR. PASTOR, BIBLE EVANGELICAL FREE CHURCH, TOMAH, WI.

EXCELLENT, powerful, very well done. I need a box of these books next week! This is not a book of theory, Gary writes from years of encouraging and equipping leaders for the revolution. He allows us to feel the rhythms and priorities that created a life-changing way of doing life together on mission. He calls us from the program-focused mind set to the integrated life of disciplemaking that exploded on the first century world. DNA of a Revolution challenges me to not play it safe.

— **STEVE HOPKINS,** *GROUP LEADER: BIBLE TEACHING AND LEADERSHIP RESOURCE GROUP, STATE CONVENTION OF BAPTISTS IN OHIO*

IKNOW Gary thinks this book is for pastors and ministry leaders, but he's wrong. *Every Christian should read it!*

— **KEN MCMULLEN**
Professor, US HISTORY NUT, SANTA ANA, CA

D NA of a Revolution is for those who believe the Church is called to be more than a critic of a deteriorating culture. It is for those concerned that the Church is becoming an island of piety in the sea of irrelevance. And, it is for those who still believe that the church remains God's chosen vehicle to reach His world with the hope of Jesus. This book you are holding will assistant anyone who recognizes that the privileged place of "church" is passing yet the need for Jesus remains. As a church leader I am picky about what I read, but this is a book that fits our time and place at our church. Gary combines biblical scholarship with practiced expertise and a heart that beats for God's church to impact our world.

— BOB THOMAS

LEAD PASTOR, CALVARY CHURCH, LOS GATOS, CA

G ARY'S insightful reflections on the Book of Acts are immensely helpful in showing the church how to navigate the waters of cultural change. As someone who has worked with hundreds of churches and ministries, Mayes urges us to reclaim the values and priorities embraced by the earliest Jesus followers. He skillfully points the way forward by having us look afresh at the revolution that once was Christianity.

— MIKE ERRE, LOVER OF ALL THINGS OHIO STATE

SENIOR PASTOR, EVANGELICAL FREE CHURCH, FULLERTON CA

G ARY Mayes' remarkably engaging interpretation of Acts deftly combines expert "man on the street" straight-talk, with the wit and color of a front-line observer of the inner workings of the church. Few authors unlock the DNA mystery of the first century revolution in a way that compels the reader to join the crowds and take to the streets to bring the dream to life! Passion for the Church is splashed on every page and compels the reader to rediscover the genetic code that will splice each of us into the grandest revolution ever imagined.

— STEVE HOKE

CO-AUTHOR, THE GLOBAL MISSION HANDBOOK; LEADERSHIP TRAINER

I'VE served on several elder boards in local churches and I only wish I had a volume like this during those days. What Gary presents gives hope and an ancient way forward. It is of immeasurable value: easy to read, biblical, and practical—wisdom accumulated over many years of passionate commitment to the local church. If I had known—and lived out—even a fraction of what he describes in The DNA of a Revolution, I could have avoided a lot of pain. This book is of superb value for any local church serious about health, vitality, and being in the center of God's missional intent for the world.

— **SAM METCALF**
President, Church Resource Ministries

THIS is provocative, challenging and encouraging. Gary doesn't just say we have a problem, but his whole train of thought is one of forward movement, contributing to the conversation in ways that are helpful and tangible. His chapter on mentoring the next generation of leaders is huge, especially for us young guys. What Gary has given us here is incredible.

— **TRAVIS COLLINS**
Director of BETA Communities, CRM, Long Beach, CA

FRESH, clear and easy to understand. This book is definitely not a regurgitation of something I have read before. I really like getting back to what Luke's tells us about the foundations and "DNA" of the Church. Let's look to the Bible to see what it tells us about the foundations of the Church—what a novel idea!

— **KYLE KALMA**
Principal, Clear Media Group: Corona, CA

SELDOM have I read a book about the Church and ministry that has motivated me more to get past the warm fuzzy feelings of inspiration to thoughtful, eager action. As I turned each page of DNA of a Revolution it was as if I was given fresh eyes for The Book of Acts and an intensified desire to be the leader that God meant for me to be, to lend leadership for what the Church was meant to be – a revolutionary community that is legitimately the hope of the world.

— **ED SALAS**
Pastor of Human Development, NewSong, Orange County, CA

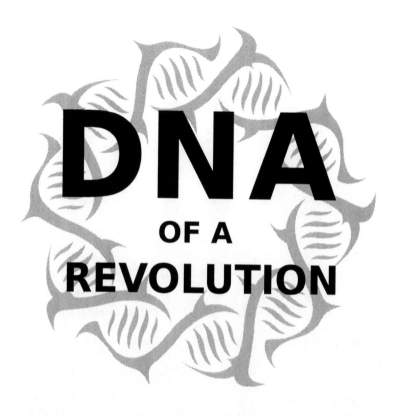

DNA
OF A
REVOLUTION

THE SMALL GROUP EXPERIENCE

1st century breakthroughs that will
transform the impact of the church

GARY MAYES

LONG WAKE
Leaving a Lasting Imprint

www.longwake.com

DNA of a Revolution: *The Small Group Experience*
© 2015 by Gary R. Mayes

ISBN-13: 978-0692438541
ISBN-10: 0692438548

First Printing: May 2015

Cover and Art Design by **Jason Loftis: http://jloft.com**

10 9 8 7 6 5 4 3 2 1

LONG WAKE

Leaving a Lasting Imprint

www.longwake.com

Lasting influence flows from the integration of who we are and what we do as followers of Jesus. Long Wake Publishing produces resources committed to both.

For
Ed Salas and Steve Hopkins

The two of you are some of God's kindest gifts to me. You are a source of constant encouragement and support. You are leaders who live with personal integrity, irresistible passion for Jesus, and world-class humility. You are Barnabas to me and to hundreds of others.

May the Lord multiply your tribe.

Contents

Introduction
to this Study Guide

DNA of a Revolution

Adventure
Imagination
Innovation
Risk
Joy
Sacrifice
Mystery
Revolution
Hope

DON'T know what words come to your mind when you think about the church that could be, but words like these describe the church I dream of. I wrote DNA of a Revolution and this companion study guide as a way of fanning into flame hopes and dreams like these. Dreams that become reality.

If you are reading this, it is probably because you have been invited to participate in a small group study that looks afresh at the book of Acts through the lens of my book, *DNA of a Revolution.* I invite you to consider this as much more than another group study. It is an invitation to re-discover the adventure of following Jesus together. It is a journey of discovery about living into the life God always intended. It is a deeper look into our DNA as the Body of Christ as it was being formed in the first century.

Allow yourself a little sanctified imagination. Picture a group discussion in the worn leather couches of your local coffee house—your favorite java-chino-soy-no-foam-one-pump-latte in hand. You and a few close friends are engaged in an unhurried conversation with the leaders of that first century church. You told them about the challenges of ministry in the present day and asked for their wisdom. What do you imagine they would say? How do you think they would respond?

Think about it. That little band of men and women began with 120 people in an upper room and became a movement that transformed the Roman world. They lived with no manual on how to be the church. They were a powerless group of persecuted outcasts. They had no models of successful churches to emulate, no seminars to attend, no books to read, and no New Testament to study. They were navigating without a map and every time they turned around, they faced another disruptive challenge. To borrow from Robert Quinn, "they were building the bridge as they walked across it."[1]

If those leaders of the first century church could speak to the church of the twenty-first century, what advice would

---

1   Robert Quinn, *Deep Change.* Jossey-Bass, 1996. p. 83.

they give us? What would they want us to know? What would they dwell on and what would they skip over?

They would tell us their story. They would tell us about the tenuous experience of figuring things out as they went. They would tell us about times of success as well as failure. They would tell us about precarious turning points that radically changed the way they did life and ministry. They would relay the stories that taught them what was important. In short, they would tell us about the events God used to establish their DNA as a church trying their best to follow Jesus and his mission.

How can I be so sure? Because, that's exactly what Luke did when he wrote the book of Acts as we know it.

And, that may be the genius of the book of Acts. Rather than telling us this is THE way and that we should copy what they did, Luke reveals the DNA that would show us how to thrive in any culture, in any context, at any time. The book of Acts is not a book of methods to be replicated, but a book whose stories tell us how we were made and what we were made for. It is time to stop asking how we can get back to the way they did things in the early church. It is time to start paying attention to the missiology and ecclesiology embedded in the stories of their journey.

Acts tells us that there were at least eight times when that early church had to go back to the drawing board and at times start over. Those turning points became the places of DNA forming breakthrough and by talking us through them, Luke shows us our DNA and, in so doing, shows us the keys to unleashing our revolutionary potential in the twenty-first century.

ACKNOWLEDGEMENTS

Before DNA of a Revolution was finished I knew that a group study guide would be forthcoming. However, without the specific help of a number of people this study guide would only be a pipe dream.

Ellen Burany, you are one of the most gifted female leaders I know. It is an honor to watch God work through you. I can't thank you enough, your initial ideas for this study guide literally got me unstuck. *Doug Humphreys*, your willingness to pilot this material with your elders and staff at Creekside was not only helpful, but very encouraging. Doug you are the real deal. *Steve Hoke*, I can't believe that you enjoy the editorial review process, but it is an amazing gift. Linking arms with you at ChurchNEXT is pure delight for me. *Jason Loftis*, your artistic skills and media savvy are only surpassed by your godly character.

A PERSONAL WORD FOR PASTORS ...

I work with pastors and ministry leaders every day and I created this study guide for them above all. We live in a day of quantum change and as leaders we need a way to invite our people into paradigm shaping discoveries that are anchored in the Scriptures. My prayer is that this book and now this study guide would give you a way to serve your people and advance the impact of your ministry.

I long to unleash a revolutionary movement of hope through the church for a lost and broken world. This is one small contribution to that dream.

Gary Mayes, April 2015

ABOUT THIS STUDY GUIDE

This study guide was written to empower small groups to dream together about the church that could be, awaken fresh longing for the impact the church could make, and unleash a new sense of adventure for what it means to be a community of Christ-followers who live on mission together. It will explore the building blocks of our DNA that were formed by the experiences of the first century.

This is not your normal study guide. Rather than a redundant review of a book to help you master the content of DNA of a Revolution, this is a companion study that has merit even for people who never read the book. It is designed to provoke fresh thinking, imagination, and even evaluation of some things that many of us take for granted. And, it will ask you to take personal action with every unit.

Taking action is powerful. Adventure happens when we step out in obedience to test and experience the insights God reveals. So, go beyond talking. Go beyond words and ideas shared in a group. Take seriously the final step of each study and do something in response. Learning and discoveries take flight when we take action.

In a group study like this, I know it is not always possible for every person to have read the book in preparation for each meeting, so each unit begins with a short review— the Backstory.

The **BACKSTORY** is a shorthand review and a provocative reminder as to why the subject of each unit is so essential. After this introductory material, each unit in the study guide will take you and your small group through four stages of discovery.

EXPLORE:

These questions are designed to help you begin personally considering some of the core concepts from the corresponding chapter of DNA of a Revolution.

EXAMINE:

This section is aimed at helping you process those core concepts in light of your current church experience and practice.

ENVISION:

Here you will turn your imagination loose and dream about what could be possible.

ENGAGE:

In this final section, you will identify attainable action step(s). Taking action unleashes new learning and new discovery. Biblically, it is the response of obedience.

Guard your time so that you don't short-change this step of action.

ONE

Riding the Rapids

BACKSTORY:

It is time to dream again

T is time to dream of what the church could be and the revolutionary impact we could make in a broken and lost world. The Good News has transformational power and we have been invited—no, actually we've been tasked—to demonstrate and deliver that news to a needy world. The challenge *and the adventure* before us is that the world around us is changing at light speed.

We live in the midst of seismic change on every level of life. The very landscape beneath our feet is changing and these changes fuel a global conversation about the way forward for the church. On every continent, ministry leaders explore questions about the nature, mission, effectiveness, and contextual relevance of the church in its current forms.

This book exists to contribute to that global conversation. While so much contemporary writing about the church addresses demographic shifts or explores successful church methods, this book is written to provoke fresh thinking about the church based on the events in the book of Acts. The journey of the early church brought them to critical turning points and junctions where they literally had to start over. Examining the formational impact of those moments reveals critical pieces of our DNA—the keys to the way forward for us in the twenty-first century.

EXPLORE:

1. Read this quote and discuss the three questions that follow.

> "It is time to reintroduce a word into the operational lexicon and expectations of the church: *revolutionary*... The way we live, as well as the words we preach, ought to serve as a revolutionary invitation and influence for the kingdom... This community of Christ followers called the church was wired to operate in our world in a manner that is life-givingly counter-cultural... We should be a people of hope who turn the world upside down as the *normal* course of business." (DNA, p. 25-26)

a. How do you personally respond to the idea of the church as a revolutionary entity?

b. How comfortable do you think the majority of people in your church would be identifying themselves as a revolutionary people?

    c. What expectations in your church might be interrupted by this notion of the Body of Christ as a revolutionary force?

2. In considering the breakthrough moments for that church in the first century, *DNA of a Revolution* references the fact that the early church had to go back to the drawing board and "start over" at least eight times.

    a. How many of the "start over" moments can you identify?

    b. If you had been part of that early church, which of those moments would you have found most disconcerting? Why?

EXAMINE:

3. Choose a number from 1 to 10 that represents where you think *your church* falls on the continuum between "safe-icon of mainstream America" (1) and "revolutionary influence in community and culture" (10)?

1......2......3......4......5......6......7......8......9......10

4. Imagine your church becoming more of a revolutionary force of Good News in your community and on your culture. What are some of the things that would have to change for that dream to become reality?

5. Think about your personal longings. If there was one area of life in your town or community that you would long for your church to influence, what would it be?

ENVISION:

6. The dream of being a church that makes a revolutionary impact in its community can elicit both excitement and apprehension.

   a. What would you find exciting?

   b. What might make you nervous or fearful?

ENGAGE:

7. Revolutionary impact rarely starts with anything more than a single first step.

   In light of the questions you have just explored, what is *one thing* you could do—one specific step you could take—in the next 2-3 days to do one new thing as a revolutionary follower of Jesus?

TWO

The Power of Mission

Acts 1:1-11

BACKSTORY:

THE movie *Braveheart* became a worldwide blockbuster, not only because of its spectacle as an epic story, but because it resonated with a common longing for a cause worthy of our lives. In my own words, the point of the movie is that without a cause worth dying for, we don't have a cause worth living for.

That cause? The redemptive agenda of Jesus that shapes our nature and mission as his people. At the center of who we are is a God-sized mission. It is so important that this is *the* starting point from which Luke told the story of the early church. The church we long for is not a pipe dream and the journey toward it begins with renewed clarity about the nature of our mission.

When Luke picked up his pen and started writing what we know as the book of Acts, he devoted page one to answering the question of what matters most. Luke opened the narrative by showing us that Jesus' final act before his ascension was to declare our central priority as the people who bear his name. Jesus chose us to carry his message of hope and life and healing into a desperate world. He chose us to tell his story. He said, "Live…as my witness… [from here] to the ends of the earth and I will empower you through my Holy Spirit as you go."[1]

We are the agents of his redemptive plan.

We are not just members of some organization Jesus started, but missionaries sent by a missionary God with a crystal clear agenda. We are missionaries, whether we live in a place called home or on the other side of the globe.

What if, instead of working on mere incremental change to our methodologies, we had a big conversation about the heart of our mission? What if we went back to the drawing board with nothing set in stone but our mission alone? How would that change the questions we ask?

On the day of Jesus' Ascension, that early church really knew only one thing with certainty. They knew their mission.

EXPLORE:

1. How do you think a typical person in your church would answer the following question? *"What is the primary thing our church is about?"*

   And, how would *you* answer it?

---

1   A slight paraphrase of Acts 1.6-8

2. Listening to the responses of the group to the first question, what is encouraging or discomforting about the answers that surfaced?

3. Read the following quote and discuss the following two questions:

> "We have a missionary God who called us to follow him on his mission in a lost and broken world... Every Christ-follower is called to a missionary life. The normal life for ordinary followers of Jesus is to live as missionaries in their everyday lives. And, as a result, every local church is a missionary outpost—a community of Christians on mission together." (DNA, p.41)

a. On a scale of 1-10, how true is this of the mindset of the majority of people in your church? (1=low; 10=high)

   1......2......3......4......5......6......7......8......9......10

b. How true is it of your own mindset?

   1......2......3......4......5......6......7......8......9......10

EXAMINE:

4. Take it a step deeper. On a heart level, (that combination of mind, emotion, and will,) what do you think keeps us from believing we are missionaries and living as such everyday?

5. Chapter Two in DNA talks about three shifts that flow out of this understanding of our mission in Acts 1:6-8. All three interrupt a certain level of familiar thought and behavior in the church.

   Here is a quick summary of those three shifts as a basis for the questions that follow.

   ### SHIFT #1: From Witness*ing* to Witness*es*

   At some point in recent decades, witnessing came to mean that confrontational style of evangelism where well-meaning people accost others in order to present them with the "plan of salvation."

   Did you notice Jesus said be my witnesses and not do witnessing? We are surrounded by opportunities to be good news and demonstrate the hope of heaven by addressing the ravages of hell right now. Being a witness is about living as someone who conversationally declares Good News as much as they live in a way that is Good News.

Shift #2: From Members to Missionaries

Membership is about rights and privileges. It is about joining and belonging. Members of an organization focus on the goods and services they receive in exchange for their membership.

We were commissioned as ambassadors of reconciliation who bring grace and truth to a fallen world. We are God's primary delivery system of hope. We are witnesses. It is a mission that is bigger than any of us. The word for people who live on mission? Missionaries.

Shift #3: From Attraction to Incarnation

In the typical American church of the past 50 years, the life of the congregation orbited around the building and we hoped other people would find what we did there to be attractive.

The time has come for us to look one another in the eye and admit that the world at our doorstep is staying away from the church on purpose.

An attractional posture means trying to get people to come to us. It assumes some level of hunger to know God and a level of trust in us. An incarnational posture means building bridges to them.

a. Which of these three shifts do you see as the biggest stretch for the people of your church? Why do you think that is?

b. Which shift has your church already made or is making significant progress on right now?

c. How are people responding to those changes?

d. What do you perceive as the biggest obstacles to gaining trust and a hearing with people in your community who do not follow Jesus?

ENVISION:

6. Let's dream of a different day. Imagine your church was a band of missionaries (whether 50, 200, or 5,000) sent to your community as the very first Christians anyone in your town had ever known.

a. What kinds of things would you do to live out your mission as witnesses—your mission to make disciples in this new land?

    b.   Where and how would you get started?

ENGAGE:

> "Jesus marked us as people called to live outside our cloistered walls of safety and in redemptive relationships with those who surround us."
> (DNA, p.37)

7. Let's make it personal. What is one step you could take during the next seven days to begin or build a potentially redemptive relationship with one person in your personal orbit who is not a Christ follower?

THREE

Getting
The Who Right
Acts 1:20-26

BACKSTORY:

ONE of the most important actions in the life of any congregation is leadership selection. Who you appoint to leadership roles will have long-term and indelible impact on the priorities, vitality, and impact of the church. It happens because influence flows out of who you are. Therefore getting the who *right* is much more important than filling empty seats at the leadership table.

The fledgling church in Acts 1 knew this to be true. As they began to address their future, the person they selected to fill the place vacated by Judas would be vitally important. Of all the considerations for what matters in a leader, the question at hand is, *what matters most? What is non-negotiable?*

When Peter stood before the congregation in Acts One, he cut through the fog of leadership complexity. While we have a tendency to make things complex and at times, "politically correct," Peter focused on three things that qualify a leader. He narrowed the entire realm of reasonable leadership competencies and responsibilities to three essentials that define what matters most in leaders of the church.

- A track record of intimacy with Jesus
- A life of witness
- A commitment to leading out of community

EXPLORE:

1. Read the quote below then discuss this question:
   How does your experience or perception of what it means to serve in church leadership compare with this description?

> "Leadership within the Body of Christ should be a different experience than that of our culture. It should be life-giving rather than soul-starving. If we are a church who embodies the Good News, then serving as a leader in any arena of church life should be an experience of good news." (DNA, p. 49)

EXAMINE:

2. When it comes to the leadership selection process in your congregation, what criteria would most members of your congregation say are essential?

3. How do those criteria compare and contrast with the three criteria identified by the Apostles for selection of the person to replace Judas?

4. On which of the three criteria do you think it is easiest to "give someone a pass?" Why do *you* think that is?

ENVISION:

5. What do you imagine some of the long-term results might be in the life of your church if leaders were chosen with these primary criteria in mind?

On the other hand, what long-term results would you imagine if leaders are chosen who do not live by these three criteria?

6. Who are some of the leaders in your church, (both formal and informal leaders,) who model these three criteria? (List their names next to each criterion.)

   a. Those whose lives are anchored in sustained communion with the Savior?

   b. Who embody a life of witness that impacts the world around them?

   c. Who live and work in collaborative partnership with others?

ENGAGE:

7. This week, affirm one of those leaders for the example and influence of their life.

   a. Who will you choose?

   b. What will you highlight about his/her life and impact?

   c. When and how will you communicate with them? (phone, letter, in person, ??)

FOUR

An Apprenticing Community

Acts 2:38-47

BACKSTORY:

PRIOR to this moment in human history, (the Day of Pentecost) every follower of Jesus had been taught directly by Jesus himself. Now, suddenly, more than 3,000 brand new followers of Christ need to be formed as disciples without Jesus to do it. Jesus is no longer here in person, so, what can this young congregation do to help all of these new believers learn to walk as Jesus walked?

This young church needed to create an environment that would disciple this ever-increasing flow of new believers into the fullness of all that it means to follow Jesus. They needed a way to develop new followers into witnesses. What emerged may not satisfy our modern desire for something we can "plug and play," but it invites us into a rhythm of life that will transform everything we do. Luke describes five dimensions of that rhythm.

In doing so, Luke shows us that the role of the Incarnate Rabbi is now shared by the community. In the same way that the Body of Christ embodies the mission of Jesus, the Body has been tasked to develop and deploy his followers. The Body of Christ is the apprenticing community—the community is the discipler.

The whole scene raises questions for us about the effectiveness of our disciple-making processes. What are we hoping to accomplish through all of our church programs? How effectively are we equipping followers of Christ to walk as Jesus walked? What matters most and what doesn't matter?

EXPLORE:

1. Consider this statement:

    "To follow Jesus was to be apprenticed not only into relationship with him, but also into a life of mission that looked like his own." (DNA, p.69)

    What are the critical components of an apprenticing process as you see it?

2. Make a quick list of the major ministry programs in the life of your church. Then, next to each program, describe the one primary thing it is designed to accomplish in the lives of your people.

major program	primary contribution

3. Looking at your list, what do you see? Any patterns?

How does your list compare to the apprenticing process you discussed a moment ago?

EXAMINE:

Each of the five dimensions of how they did life together in the first century interrupts at least one dimension of contemporary church thought and practice. We don't have time in this study to look at all five, but we can look closely at two of them.

4. *"Devotion to the Apostles teaching."*

"This devotion meant so much more than our current focus on teaching as the acquisition of biblical content. In the Western world today, we believe teaching has happened when the teacher has covered his or her material. In the ancient world—and most of the non-Western world today—teaching has not happened until the student has acted on what they were taught. Devotion to the apostles' teaching in this context has as much to do with obedience as it does to understanding." (DNA, p.72)

a. How would a commitment to putting everything we are taught into immediate action transform the typical approaches to Bible study you've been part of?

b. What changes would a constant commitment to action bring to other programs in the life of your church?

c. Getting really personal: each of these studies has included specific action steps. How has that gone for you and the people in your small group? Are people completing their action steps?

5. **"Generosity for anyone in need"**

> "When God is at work in his people, there is a consistent pattern of engagement with the poor and marginalized. His heart for the poor shows up throughout the Scriptures. So it should come as no surprise that here, in the earliest days of life in the church, God's heart for the poor is normalized into their ongoing pattern of life."
> (DNA, p. 75)

a. On a scale of 1-10, how often do you think the people of your church identify with and sacrificially care for the poor and marginalized as a *normal* part of life? (1=rarely; 10=constantly)

1......2......3......4......5......6......7......8......9......10

b. How would you rate yourself on the same scale?

1......2......3......4......5......6......7......8......9......10

c. While attention to the other practices in Acts 2:42ff. is usually seen as essential for every believer, it seems that consistent "generosity for the poor" is something we treat as a bit negotiable.

Why do you think that happens?

What would it take to change that perspective?

ENVISION:

6. If we had the courage to go back to the drawing board and design church life as an apprenticing environment which integrates these five rhythms of Acts 2, what do you think we could do?

   How could we intentionally cultivate all five rhythms without adding more to the church "calendar?"

ENGAGE:

7. Considering your own development as an apprentice of Jesus—as a disciple—what is one thing that stood out to you during this study that calls for more attention?

   What is one concrete step of response you will take this week?

FIVE

More than an Organism

Acts 6.1-7

BACKSTORY:

THE ongoing and rapid growth of the early church created serious growing pains. By the time we get to the events of Acts 6, it would be safe to guesstimate the size of this first congregation at twenty to twenty-five thousand or more.[1]

Even if these numbers are off by a large margin, what is clear is that this young church was nothing like the warm intimate group of 120 that used to meet in the upper room. (Acts 1.15) Yet, they still had the original leadership structure and personnel established in chapter one.

---

1 Acts 4.4 reports that the size of the church numbered about five thousand men and Luke tells us that the church continued to grow. And, although it was the custom of the time to number the size of a group by counting the number of men, we know there would have been a significant number of women and children in addition to the men.)

The capacity for growth and sustainable impact for any movement relates directly to its effectiveness at developing appropriate and responsive organizational structures. The church is no exception. We speak often of the church as an organism. However, many fail to grasp that organization and organism complement rather than compete with one another. The early church discovered the role of healthy structures when an organizational meltdown nearly derailed everything.

These days, it seems that as often as not, organizational structures in the church hinder the church's mission and drain the life of its leaders. Rather than developing revolutionaries, we nurture bureaucrats. Rather than increasing our capacity for ministry impact, our systems and structures consume human capital. Rather than empowering workers and leaders with the authority and resources they need to initiate kingdom-focused ministry, unhealthy structures frustrate and constrain people. In Acts 6, we get to see courageous leaders tackle the challenge of organizational life head on.

EXPLORE:

1. "We speak often of the church as an organism. However, many fail to grasp that organization and organism complement rather than compete with one another." (DNA, p. 85)

a. What do you think most people mean when they say that the church is an organism not an organization?

b. What is it about an organism that feels more desirable than an organization?

2. Acts 6 tells us Greek widows weren't getting food. It was an accusation of *institutionalized racism!*

   If you'd been there as a leader in that church, what would your instinctive response have been? How would you have addressed the problem?

3. The Apostles saw that they had an organizational breakdown. Read the following statement and talk about a time where you saw this principle lived out.

   > "When organizational systems and structures break down, waves of impact affect people in ways we are not aware of. When you have good people with good intentions attempting to do good work and yet, in the process keep hurting one another, you have broken systems."
   > (DNA, p. 87)

EXAMINE:

4. Read the following quote and then discuss the questions that follow.

> "If the early church had the freedom to tamper with the leadership structure Jesus himself instituted, we are on good ground to evaluate and experiment with organizational approaches that might work better in our context."
> (DNA, p. 99)

a. What are the sacred cows in your church— organizational structures, congregational processes, even some programs—that you think people would never agree to change?

b. If you had no fear of making a mistake what is it about the way your church operates that you would like to try differently?

ENVISION:

5. Let's try the Acts 2 test.
Imagine that when you arrive for services this coming weekend, your congregation has suddenly and permanently quadrupled in size.

Picturing that scenario in your mind, take a shot at answering this sample of predictable organizational questions that would arise:

a. What is it about the way your church is structured that will not work with that many people?

b. How will your decision-making processes need to be altered?

c. How does communication within your congregation happen now, and how will that need to be changed to effectively communicate with all these new people?

d. How will new leaders be developed and empowered with the authority they need to lead this many people?

e. How will you apprentice all these people tp love Jesus and live on mission with abandon?

f. [After working through these questions, see the final note in this unit for an insight into why this "test" has so much power.]

ENGAGE:

6. In your conversation around the "Acts 2 test" did any significant ideas or insights surface that should be offered to the senior leadership of the church?

To whom should you share your ideas? And, who would be the best spokesperson for your group?

7. Leadership is tough business.
   Hebrews 13.17 says, *"Have confidence in your leaders and submit to their authority. They keep watch over you as those who must give an account. Do this so that their work will be a joy, not a burden, for that would be of no advantage to you."*

   Having talked about the importance of organizational matters, would you covenant to pray for the leaders of your church every day this next week?

About the "Acts 2 Test"

No one really knows what would be needed if their church instantly quadrupled in size. However, the very exercise of trying to imagine that scenario causes people to recognize organizational issues that need to be addressed right now. Those issues that surface for you when you ask these questions are probably barriers already hindering the transformational potential of your church today.

SIX

Explosive Multiplication

Acts 8.1-8

BACKSTORY:

> "On that day a great persecution broke
> out against the church
> at Jerusalem and *all* except the
> apostles were *scattered* throughout
> Judea and Samaria." (Acts 8.1)

THE first church lost its entire congregation! This amazing community—those people who shared everything—saw the sweet season of those early days destroyed. No longer could they meet in the beautiful courtyard of the temple. No longer could they meet in one another's homes. Familiar rhythms of life and the life-giving gatherings of this church were finished. Relationships were torn apart. They had to start over.

The unexpected twist in the story is that the persecution backfired. Just when we modern-day readers begin to appreciate the substance of their sorrow, Luke reveals something none of us would have expected. Saul set out to extinguish the church, but instead, this persecution unleashed a church-planting explosion. Instead of destroying the church, he succeeded in deploying the members of this congregation throughout all of Israel and Samaria and beyond. They did not scatter and hide. Members of that first congregation became missionaries.

There may be few other places in the book of Acts where the gap between what happened then and what we experience today is greater. It seems like quite a stretch to think that if we scattered every member of our churches, every one of them would instinctively start introducing new people to Jesus and mobilizing them into new churches.

What would it take? What would it take to normalize the frequent multiplication of new churches and large-scale participation in the disciplemaking process that undergirds it? What would it take to shift from thinking about church as gathering to church as going? What would it take to make the deployment of Christians as witnesses the new normal instead of perpetually providing Christians with more theological content?

EXPLORE:

1. The persecution that arose in Acts 8 forced the *entire* congregation to flee from Jerusalem. It effectively closed the church. But, what everyone did next was quite amazing. Consider...

Acts 8.4 tells us that *"all those who were scattered preached the word wherever they went."* The normal life of those early believers was to make new disciples.

> "Discipleship is ultimately not about the acquisition of biblical facts, compliance with church doctrine, or the cultivation of common religious practices. For too long we have divorced any sense of engagement 'out there' from our expectations for a normal Christ-follower." (DNA, p. 116-117)

a. From your perspective, how would you summarize what most churches expect from their people as the normal Christian life?

b. What do you think are some of the biggest hurdles that keep people from embracing a life of engagement with lost and broken people as the normal Christian life?

EXAMINE:

2. In Acts 8.5-8 Luke describes the adventures of one of those scattered believers. Philip went to an unnamed town in Samaria where he not only "proclaimed the Messiah," but cast out demons and healed many. The resulting impact of his ministry was, *"There was great joy in the city."*

Read the following statement and then discuss the questions below.

> "It is time to deconstruct our notions of witness as obligation and discover that participation in the mission of Jesus is the path to joy. Living as a witness, engaging with people in a way that brings healing to the brokenness and evil in our world, and establishing new churches in order to multiply those efforts is so much more than a matter of duty. It is the pathway to joy. Theirs and ours!" (DNA, p. 109)

a. In your church, how foreign or familiar is the concept of bringing joy to your city?

b. What are some ways church planting could bring joy to a city?

c. What are some of the aspects of life in your community—areas of brokenness and injustice—that need the healing presence of Jesus?

ENVISION:

3. Suppose the leaders of your church announced a bold vision to plant five new churches next year. And, assume that all of the manpower and resources to carry out this plan had to come from within your current congregation.

   a. What would your first reaction be?

   b. What fears would surface in you regarding planting that many new churches?

   c. What would it take to succeed at that kind of church multiplication?

   d. What would need to change in your church for you to succeed?

   e. How would pursuing a vision like this change you?

4. Five new churches next year might be unrealistic, but what do you think it would take for your church to start the process of planting one new church that was focused on making new disciples from the harvest?

ENGAGE:

5. Challenge yourselves as a group (whoever you are doing this study with.) Where could you began engaging in ministry as witnesses in your city? You could become an instrument of joy for others.

    > "Deploying people into the harvest is as much a part of their formation as what happens in the disciplines of solitude... the small groups and/ or classes in your church [can become] learning communities that engage a broken world around you as much as they focus on teaching new information."
    > (DNA, p. 117)

    a. What could you do as a small group to live out the Good News in your community? *(You don't have to make a permanent commitment, but take a first few steps. Experiment together.)*

    b. Who will take the lead for your group and what first steps will you take this week?

IDENTIFYING OPPORTUNITIES

It is not uncommon for people to wonder where and how to get started. Therefore, consider these questions as a way to help you identify an opportunity:

- What is one need in your city that you feel motivated to meet?

- Are there any groups of people in your community with whom you already have some connection? (Civic groups, civic initiatives, schools, sports or hobby groups, business associations, etc. For more see the section on "people groups" in DNA: pp.114-115)

- Is there a specific person or family known by someone in your group who needs real help.

- Is there an organization trying to meet a need in your city where you could volunteer?

SEVEN

Diversity: Heaven in the Present

Acts 10-11

BACKSTORY

WHAT started with prayer, turned into a nap, and then became a vision that changed the course of the church forever.

You know the story of Peter's vision in Acts 10. Three times a banquet was placed in front of him filled with foods that he would never eat as a devout Jewish man. But the vision wasn't really about food, it was about God's heart and mission for all mankind.

> "God has shown me that I should not call anyone impure or unclean... I now realize how true it is that God does not show favoritism but accepts those from every nation who fear him and do what is right." (Acts 10.28, 34-35)

Left to our human nature, we tend toward bubbles of socioeconomic isolation. We choose to associate with people like us. We find comfort with those who look at life the way we do, affirm our opinions, and share our world view. But, a ghettoized church does not look like the world we are called to reach, and worse, does not reflect God's heart. Jesus was not a blond-haired, blue-eyed, Westerner. Neither was he a champion of our preferred political party. God's mission in the world encompasses every tribe, every people, every nation, and every political persuasion without exception.

EXPLORE:

1. What is one story of either your most delightful or awkward experience with a person (or a group of people) from another culture?

2. Read the following paragraphs aloud, then discuss the questions below:

   > "Peter's rooftop vision and corresponding obedience released a new strand of DNA into our destiny as the Body of Christ. In a prophetic way, this way of life stands in contrast with the persistent hostility of mankind against itself. By the way we embrace people who are different than we are, we interrupt the abusive patterns of the world and put Good News on display.
   >
   > Jesus unleashes his church as a beacon of hope in a world practiced at intolerance. He commissions us to live out the welcoming embrace of heaven amidst the hellish injustice of the present.

The heart of God reaches beyond everything
that divides men and women. The mission and
the heart God obliterate everything we use to
marginalize people." (DNA, p.127)

a. What are some reasons you can think of for
why diversity can be hard for local churches?

b. What are some of the messages a culturally
and ethnically diverse church sends to its
community?

EXAMINE:

3. Looking at your community, what group(s) of
people are under represented in your church?
*(Think broadly to include any group of different ethnicity,
culture, socioeconomic status, political persuasion, age, etc.)*

4. Has the issue of diversity been talked about
in your church? What are some of the issues
that might be good for your leaders and your
congregation to discuss?

5. Considering the groups of people who are under-represented in your congregation, think about the rhetoric, the announcements, the ways of talking about life in your church.

    a. Does your language tend to be inviting and welcoming to everyone? Are there any times when language and labels might cause people to feel marginalized? What are some examples of both?

    b. Imagine you had a good friend and co-worker visiting your church for the first time, who also happened to be from one of those under-represented groups you listed above. Is there anything about their experience you might be nervous about?

ENVISION:

6. As a starting point, what people group(s) might be within the easiest reach of your church? What group(s) do you sense God drawing you toward?

    a. What would it take to build bridges to that group? *(For additional ideas, see the "Starting Points" section in DNA. pp. 129ff.)*

b. What would that group add to the life of your
congregation?

c. Moving out of that comfort zone of hanging
with people like us can feel threatening. What
hurdles will your church have to overcome to
become enthusiastic about diversity?

ENGAGE:

7. Considering all that is involved in moving toward
greater diversity, is there anything you need to
confess or repent?

Take time to reflect and make notes of the things
you hear the Spirit of God saying to you. Then
as a group take time to pray these prayers of
confession.

EIGHT

Decision Making and Authority

Acts 13.1-3

BACKSTORY:

BEFORE Acts 13, the center of gravity for the church was anchored in Jerusalem. After the events of Acts 13, everything shifted. It all happened because a group of courageous leaders was adept at listening for and responding to the leadership of the Spirit.

Our familiarity with the history of the Church in the New Testament makes it easy to take the missionary journeys of Paul and Barnabas for granted. However, the decision to send out these two missionaries was anything but benign. Prior to this moment, Christianity was a regional presence on the eastern edges of the Mediterranean. This was the first intentional deployment of "vocational missionaries" in history.

What gave them the authority, not to mention the audacity, to make and act on such a decision? What gave them the right to do something that could shape the perception of Christianity throughout the Roman Empire? Who gave them the authority to send these two men on a potentially life-threatening journey?

The essence of decision making in the Body of Christ boils down to seeking and following the active leadership of the Spirit. We can trust him to lead us. The truth is, he loves to speak to us far more than we like to listen.

This practice of listening-obeying obliterates any notion of church life as a static experience of religious rituals. It is a high-risk adventure of faith as the Spirit guides us into the fullness of the life and mission of Jesus. We should be on the lookout for his prompting to try what we have never tried before. We should expect him to suggest new approaches that just might extend our impact in the world. Just as the Holy Spirit spoke to the church in Antioch and asked them to deploy Barnabas and Saul in a way no one had ever done before, he continues to lead his people to take new steps that will radically advance the mission of Jesus in our contemporary world.

EXPLORE:

1. Read this paragraph outloud:

> "Leadership is more than wise planning executed by competent individuals—there is always another player in the room. His direction is what matters most. As a result, serving as a leader in the body of Christ should be a constant adventure of following the dynamic leadership of the Spirit." (DNA, p. 141)

a. Have you ever been part of a church or ministry team where you experienced that "adventure of following the leadership of the Spirit?" What was that like?

b. What are some ways you think the Spirit "speaks up" in a group? What have you learned about recognizing his voice?

2. Read this paragraph out loud and then discuss the questions below.

> "Listening and obeying are not only fundamental to following Jesus personally—they define the essence of daily practice for the community of leaders who are entrusted with the responsibility for shepherding a local church. Paul's admonition that we walk in step with the Spirit applies to the way we live as a community just as much as it does to us individually." (DNA, p. 141 and Gal. 5.25)

a. Do you agree or disagree? Why?

b. What are some ways this kind of leadership would shape the life of a local church? And, in what ways could it be disconcerting?

EXAMINE:

3. Considering some of the classic disciplines that enhance spiritual discernment—worship, fasting, listening prayer, faith-based obedience, etc.—in what areas are you strong and in what areas would you like to grow?

   a. ... Personally?

   b. ... In the ministry team you serve on?

   c. ... As a church?

ENVISION:

4. What do you think leadership meetings could be like if people were deliberately listening for the Spirit's directives together? Practically speaking, how do you think you would spend your time?

5. Following the Spirit doesn't mean dismantling everything that is familiar, but it does mean being open to his fresh leading. Consider:

   "The nature of organizations is to preserve status quo, avoid risk, move toward the lowest common denominator, and choose a path that ruffles the fewest feathers.

Responsive obedience includes being open to what is new, unknown, or untried. Without an openness to what might be new, we live with filters that only reinforce what already exists. Without openness to something untried, Barnabas and Saul might have stayed in Antioch serving the church there." (DNA, p. 149)

a. How comfortable or uncomfortable would you say your church is with new, untested, even risky ideas?

b. Can you think of any ideas, plans, or opportunities, you think the Spirit has been wanting your church to pursue? How do you think they might advance the kingdom?

c. Is there anyone in your church's leadership you should humbly share these ideas with?

ENGAGE:

6. What have you heard the Spirit saying to you about how you might listen more intentionally for his direction? *(At home, at work, or wherever.)*

What first step will you take?

NINE

Contextualization and Courage

Acts 15

BACKSTORY:

I N Acts 15, Luke tells us that a huge debate erupted when some men from Judea traveled to Antioch and started teaching on the necessity of circumcision. Most of us in the twenty-first century have a hard time relating to the question of circumcision as an emotionally charged crisis. For one thing, the issue was resolved way back then. For another, since we did not grow up in first century Israel, we don't empathize with the importance of maintaining our Jewish identity during an era of military occupation.

As the cause of Christ expanded further throughout the Roman world, Jewish believers must have struggled with the feeling that their heritage was slipping away. However, success in reaching non-Jews brought change to everything that was historically meaningful. New believers poured into the church without an appreciation for the Jewish feasts, kosher laws, or even the meaningful music of the synagogue.

Most of us can understand the ethos of their tension. Our relationship with God and our experience of his presence intertwines with the practices and traditions of our church life. Certain forms of worship and patterns of life that we learned to cherish during our young adulthood or the early years after we came to Christ will always be the most meaningful. In some cases, the forms of our Christian experience feel inseparable from our theology.

When our preferred pattern of church life changes we grieve its loss. When the style of our worship gatherings are altered it feels like the substance of our faith is compromised. When the music that leads us into the presence of the Father most meaningfully gets tossed for some new style we don't appreciate, it is easy to believe that something irreplaceable was lost. Yes, we understand that the forms we find meaningful and the substance of our faith are not the same thing. But, they often feel inextricable.

Surely, someone must draw a line in the sand at some point. Right? Should we not set a limit as to how much could or should be changed to accommodate outsiders?

EXPLORE:

1. What are some of the changes in our culture and maybe even in your local area that leave you nostalgic for the past?

2. Read the following paragraph and discuss this question: *what do you see as the major challenges to contextualizing Christianity for the culture of today?*

> "The job of ministry leaders is to translate the Gospel and the forms through which it is expressed into every context in every generation in ways that 'do not make it difficult for [those] who are turning to God.' Leaders are called to champion the dynamic process of courageous contextualization in order to advance the Gospel."
> (DNA, p. 164)

EXAMINE:

3. How would the average member of your church respond to this statement:

> "If the church of the first century was right to set aside circumcision in order to serve the advancement of the Gospel, then none of our current forms or programs or styles of doing ministry are non-negotiable. None of the ways we do church hold a candle to the longevity or God-appointed stature of circumcision."
> (DNA, p. 165)

4. How would you personally respond to the following questions?

   a. *"How far should we go in adapting our methods in order to connect with our culture?*

    b. *How would you know we have crossed the line and gone too far?*

    c. *Core doctrine aside, what specific programs or practices need to not be changed?* (DNA, p. 153)

5. What discussions or disagreements about ministry strategy and style does your church seem to get stuck on? Why do you think that is?

ENVISION:

6. Take all you know about the heart and mission of Jesus and imagine that he moved into your community this week.

    a. … what would he do first?

    b. … who are the people he would try to connect with?

    c. … where would he go and where would he "hang out?"

d. … what are some of the things he would address?

7. What might happen if your church started doing some of those things?

ENGAGE:

8. Surrender:

a. Are there any aspects of church tradition or personal preference that you personally hold onto too tightly?

b. Are there any moments when you might have stood in the way of changes that could have enhanced your church's impact?

c. Take time to surrender those meaningful preferences to the Lord. Give your wants and needs to him and trust him to care for you. Invite him to show you in a fresh way how you might contribute to shaping the church.

TEN

Generation NEXT

BACKSTORY:

EVERY generation of established leaders carries the responsibility to develop and empower the generations following behind them. Established leaders hold the keys to a new day. They have the opportunity to raise up, apprentice, and partner with leaders from the very generations we are most worried about. When we raise up those emerging leaders, they will lead the way to reach the generations we are currently losing. Those of us who are getting older do not need to become more hip or more clever in order to reach younger generations. We need to hand the keys to leaders from those generations and let them lead us.

The first century church faced the same challenge. The first generation of leaders was apprenticed directly by Jesus or by those who were. As time went by and the church spread, new leaders were needed. Who would carry the mantle in the generations to come? How were those next generations of leaders to be developed? As that first generation aged and as many of them paid the ultimate price for following Jesus, who would take their places?

The answer for the first century and for today is demonstrated by one of the most influential leaders of the New Testament. Most Christians know his name, but I think he deserves more recognition for his contribution than he generally receives. A good argument can be made that his fingerprints are on two-thirds of the New Testament books. His given name was Joe. We know him as Barnabas.

Luke makes a point to detail the pattern of Barnabas' approach with an emerging leader named Saul. In one setting after another, over a span of years, the role of Barnabas in Saul's development paints a picture of what leadership mentoring can look like. Call it mentoring, call it apprenticing, call it anything you like, but the point is the same. One man gave himself to the development of another and the kingdom exploded as a result.

EXPLORE:

1. It has been said, *"Christianity is never more than one generation away from extinction."* How would you assess the depth of the young leadership bench in your church?

2. Have you had a Barnabas? If so, what was their impact on your life?

EXAMINE:

3. As you consider your own life, how much energy are you giving to identifying, developing, and empowering younger leaders?

   a. If you are, what are you learning from the leaders you are investing yourself in?

   b. If you are not, what keeps you from doing so?

4. One of the greatest hurdles that keeps mentoring from happening broadly is our belief in one or more of these Mentoring Myths:

YODA MYTH:	*A mentor must be some über-wise sage*
GEEZER MYTH:	*Mentors must be significantly older.*
STRUCTURE MYTH:	*Mentoring equals a weekly meeting.*
GURU MYTH:	*You have one great mentor for life.*
MIND-READING MYTH:	*The right mentor or mentoree will "just know" they should approach you.*

   a. Which of these myths have held you back? In what ways?

   b. Which of the myths do you think are prevalent in your church?

   c. Can you think of any other myths that get in the way of healthy mentoring relationships?

ENVISION:

5. Consider the four stages of a mentoring partnership modeled by Barnabas:

1. SEEK OUT	*The mentor pursues potential mentoree*
2. SPONSOR IN	*The mentor leverages their personal network to open doors for the mentoree*
3. SERVE TOGETHER	*Mentor and mentoree work on project or other assigment together*
4. SEND OFF	*Mentoree "graduates" and becomes peer with mentor*

a. Have you taken any of these steps in your efforts to mentor others? What fruit came from your efforts?

b. Are any of these four stages unclear to you in any way? If so, talk as a group about what they would look like in a mentoring relationship. (see DNA pp. 174-180, for more info.)

6. What kind of impact would it make in your church if everyone in a position of leadership was actively mentoring others?

ENGAGE:

7. Who would benefit from you taking on a Barnabas-like role in their life?

What will you do to contact them this week?

ELEVEN

Spiritual Power

BACKSTORY:

IF the latest technology, great programs, professional staff, and world class buildings were enough to get the job done, the impact of the Western church in the twenty-first century would make the events recorded in Acts seem like tired cable channel reruns. The question is, where do we find true spiritual power that will make the kind of lasting impact we long for the church to make?

The answer?

Prayer.

We could devote endless energy trying to dissect the nuances of prayer: however, the point is that the early church lived a life of prayer and their prayer life is inseparable from their spiritual power. Without ever shifting into a transactional posture, they prayed in ways that call us to a life of prayer that is revolutionary. Constant. Bold. Supernaturally focused. Action oriented. They prayed and the world was changed. It is not an equation that produces the right results if we plug the right pieces in. Things happen when God's people pray that do not happen when they don't.

Their prayer life demonstrated desperate dependency on the hand of the King without crossing the line and treating God like a vending machine.

EXPLORE:

1. What thoughts and reactions are provoked in you by the following paragraph?

   "We need to be honest. No Christian would argue against the value of prayer, but in practice we often relegate it to the role of a ceremonial or sideline activity. So many other things are urgent and important. We rarely look to prayer as the most important or most strategic work of kingdom advancement. It is acknowledged as powerful, but treated as a religiously tame ritual. We could not be more wrong.

   Prayer might be the least tame thing we ever do!" (DNA, p. 189)

2. Read this quote and discuss question below.

   "Paul wrote that God uses the foolish things to confound the wise. What could be more foolish in the twenty-first century than to make a claim that prayer may be the strategic path to change the world?" (DNA, p. 202; 1 Cor. 1.27-28)

   What are some of the reasons prayer could seem "foolish" to the world?

EXAMINE:

3. Look up and read aloud the prayer of Acts 4.23-30. How does the way they prayed there compare and contrast with the way typical prayer sounds in your church?

4. If you were to evaluate the prayer-life and practices of your church, what grade would you give yourselves in these areas? (use "A-F" scale) And, why?

    a. The amount of time spent in prayer when leaders gather? ____

    b. The work of a dedicated intercession team for your church? ____

    c. The number of people who participate on any kind of prayer team? ____

    d. The number of men who participate in prayer gatherings/efforts? ____

    e. The practice of prayer in your small groups? ____

    f. The training and mentoring of your people into deeper prayer lives? ____

ENVISION:

5. Read the following paragraph and answer this question: *If we fully owned the truth of these statements, what would change about the prayer life of our church?*

> "If we could see reality through God's eyes, we would discover that what we see in the natural realm is only a small fraction of reality. If we could see reality from God's perspective, we would instantly and forever understand that we "do not struggle against flesh and blood, but against the rulers...authorities...powers of this dark world and against the spiritual forces of evil in the heavenly realms."
> (DNA, p. 194, Eph. 6:12)

6. The book of Acts records at least eight times that God supernaturally visited his people during times of prayer. Prayer is not a transactional mechanism, but at the same time, let yourself dream a little.

    a. What would it be like for your church if God began answering prayer in direct and unmistakable ways?

    b. What would that do for your people?

    c. How might it impact the life, mission, and impact of your church?

ENGAGE:

7. What surfaced in this conversation about prayer that you think should be considered in your church?

8. What has been stirred up in you that provoked ways you want to grow in your own prayer life?

TWELVE

Reclaiming our Birthright

BACKSTORY:

THROUGHOUT this study and throughout *DNA of a Revolution*, I have argued for the very nature of our birthright as a revolutionary force intended to transform the world. I do not mean revolutionary as in a frenzied crowd of angry students at a political rally, but a counter cultural, life-giving community that brings a redemptive presence into a desperate world.

A loving God who desperately loves us and loves the world invites us to join him in doing what matters most in that world and, in the process, to discover what matters most in life. Living for the sake of other people just makes sense. The allure of self-serving environments focused on "caring for me" never live up to their seductive promise.

The biblical picture is that Christians are followers of Christ; followers of Christ are disciples; and disciples are missionaries. Choose your label, they all refer to the one and only life Jesus intended. Extend the implications of that reality and you find that to be his church is to be a community of missionaries deployed into the world for the sake of the world. Anything other than that is a counterfeit.

EXPLORE:

1. What thoughts and questions surface in you when read this quote.

   > "If your church is full of members,
   > you get an occasional missionary.
   > If your church is full of missionaries,
   > the rest is just about geography."
   > (Erwin McManus)

2. Throughout this study we have talked about the revolutionary life Jesus invites us into. How does that move you deep down? Read the following paragraph and talk about what this means to you emotionally—what it means deep down in your soul.

   > "Our birthright as Children of God goes beyond a relationship with the Father to include joining him in the redemptive plan for which Jesus gave his life. Our birthright as Children of God is defined not only by restored intimacy with our creator, but is equally an invitation into partnership with him in the work that matters more than anything else on the planet."
   > (DNA, p. 209)

EXAMINE:

3. Take a few minutes to think about all that you've learned, explored and discussed in this study.

   a. What have you heard the Spirit of God saying you?

   b. Are there any personal priorities God is asking you to shift? How?

   c. Are there any patterns or beliefs that you need to repent of?

   d. Any other steps of obedience He is calling you to take?

4. All of this emphasis on mission does not mean that the church should not care for its own. We are called to love one another, to build one another up, etc.

   What are some of the ways you can imagine your church integrating a commitment to care for people with a commitment to deploy them into the world?

ENVISION:

5. As you have journeyed your way through these studies, what have you begun to dream of for your church?

6. How would you describe the impact you long to see your church make in your community?

ENGAGE:

7. Consider:

    "Every Christ-follower is called to a missionary life. The normal life for ordinary followers of Jesus is to live as missionaries in their everyday lives." (DNA, p. 41)

    What is one permanent shift you will make in order to live this missionary life everyday?

About the Author

Gary Mayes, D.Min, serves as Executive Director of ChurchNEXT for Church Resource Ministries (CRM). In this role, he leads the work of more than 100 staff on fourteen pioneering teams who work worldwide to help leaders and churches succeed in making disciples and transforming their communities.

Gary's core calling is to work with ministry leaders to help them mobilize the church to live on mission. He consults with local congregations and denominational leaders toward that end. He also speaks, trains, and leads workshops on the underlying issues that empower people and organizations to move into a life of mission.

This Study Guide is Gary's fifth book and will soon be joined by an updated edition of his book, *Now What? Resting in the Lord when Life Doesn't Make Sense.*

Gary writes a blog dedicated to the lessons about life and leadership they never taught us in school. *www.aboutleading.com.*

For inquiries about speaking engagements, training workshops, or more write to *info@garymayes.me.*

CRM EMPOWERING LEADERS

CHURCH Resource Ministries is a global movement that empowers leaders to revitalize the impact of the Church, take new ground beyond the reach of the existing church, and bring transformation among the poor—so that, disciples are made and communities are transformed.

More than 500 CRM missionaries live and minister in urban, suburban, and rural settings around the world. We believe that a different future is possible and that the Church is key to God's strategy for that redemptive potential. Our mission is inspired by a passion for the Church *that is* as well as a vision for the Church *that can be*. Our work is carried out by staff who seek to minister out of the primary values of character, relationship, competency, and spiritual passion. The heart of our strategy is developing leaders committed to both.

Since beginning in 1980, CRM has expanded to more than 30 nations and launched partner organizations led by national leaders in ten countries.

For more about CRM: www.crmleaders.org.

41178749R00060

Made in the USA
Middletown, DE
05 March 2017